Easy

Golf Courses

All Players Welcome

This book lists nearly 600 Golf Courses throughout England, Wales and Scotland which welcome all golfers.

Unless specifically mentioned, handicap certificates are not required and casual dress is acceptable.

All the courses listed were asked to approve the details given prior to publication.

The information is of necessity condensed, but in most cases telephone numbers are available should further information be required.

The weekend green fee rate usually also applies on Bank Holidays.

OTHER BOOKS PUBLISHED BY THE FORGE PRESS

Wake Up Your Memory
ISBN 0 9521328 0 X
A Concise and Practical Guide to Improving Your Memory

The Phantom Tigers
ISBN 0 9521328 1 8
A Tiger Adventure Story for Children

Easy Access

Golf Courses

All Players Welcome

Compiled by

Susan Higginson

The Forge Press

© Susan Higginson 1998

Published by The Forge Press
The Old Forge
Holton, Wincanton
Somerset, England BA9 8AX

ISBN 0 9521328 2 6

British Library Cataloguing-in-Publication Data
A catalogue record for this book
is available from the British Library.

Printed in Great Britain by Whittle Print,
Sherborne, Dorset.

Typeset by Susan Higginson

CONTENTS

Alphabetically by Counties & Administrative Areas

Name & Address	Holes/Yards Description	Green Fee	Driving Range	Facilities etc.
Beadlow Manor Hotel, Golf & Country Club Beadlow Nr Shefford 01525 860800	18/6619 18/6072 Parkland	£15 £22 Wd £20 £33 We	Yes	Full Catering Bars
Colmworth Mill Cottage New Rd, Colmworth 01234 378181	18/6559 9 Par 3 Meadowland	£6 M - W 310 Th, Fr £15 We	No	Restaurant
Mount Pleasant Station Rd Stondon Henlow 01462 850999	9 (18 tees) 6003 Meadowland	£6 Wd £8 We (9) £10.50/ £14.50 (18)	No	Snacks Bar
Mowsbury Cleat Hill Kimbolton Rd Bedford 01234 771041	18 6514 Parkland		Yes	Meals Snacks Drinks
Stockwood Park Stockwood Park London Rd Luton 01582 413704	18 6049 Meadowland	£7.30 Wd £9.60 We	Yes	Breakfast Lunch
Wyboston Lakes Wyboston 01480 223004	18 5310 Parkland	£11 Wd £15 We	No	Full Catering Golf: Book at W/e

Name & Address	Holes/Yards Description	Green Fee	Driving Range	Facilities etc.
Bird Hills Drift Rd Hawthorn Hill Nr Maidenhead 01628 771030	18 6176 Parkland	£12 Wd £15 We	Yes	Full Catering Bar
Blue Mountain Golf Centre Wood Lane Binfield 01344 300 200	18 6097 Parkland	£16 Wd £20 We	Yes	Restaurant Bar
Deanwood Park Stockcross Newbury 01635 48772	9 2200 Parkland	£7 Wd £9 We	Yes	Catering Available
Donnington Grove Country Club Grove Rd Donnington, Newbury 01635 581000	18 7050 Moorland/ Parkland	£15 Wd £25 We £5 Day Member	No	Japanese Restaurant
Donnington Valley Hotel Oxford Rd Donnington, Newbury 01635 550464	18 4215 Parkland		No	Full Catering
Downshire Easthampstead Park Wokingham 01344 302030	18 6382 Parkland		Yes	Full Catering Golf: Book 6/7 days ahead
Hurst Sandford Lane Hurst 01734 345143	9 3154 Parkland		No	Bar Booking Advisable
Lavender Park Golf Centre Swinley Rd Ascot 01344 884074	9 1124 Parkland	£3.25 Wd £4.50 We	Yes	Lunch Buffets on request Bar
Mapledurham Chazey Heath Mapledurham Reading 0118 9463353	18 5624 Parkland	£14 Wd £17 We	No	Restaurant Bar
Newbury Golf Centre The Racecourse Newbury 01635 551464	18 6249 Parkland	£10 Wd £12.50 We	Yes	Catering Available

Name & Address	Holes/Yards Description	Green Fee	Driving Range	Facilities etc.
Abbey Hill Monks Way Two Mile Ash Stony Stratford Milton Keynes 01908 562566	18 6143 Meadowland		Yes	Meals Snacks Bar
Aylesbury Golf Centre Hulcott Lane Bierton Aylesbury 01296 393644	9 2744 Parkland	£9 Wd £10 We (18 holes)	Yes	Restaurant Bar
Aylesbury Park Oxford Rd Aylesbury 01296 399196	18 6146 Parkland		No	Snacks
Aylesbury Vale Stewkley Rd Wing Leighton Buzzard 01525 240196	18 6622 Parkland	£12 Wd £18.50 We	Yes	Snacks Bars Proper golf dress Book ahead
Chalfont Park Bowles Farm Three House Holds Chalfont St Giles 01494 876293	18 5800 Parkland		Yes	Full Catering
Chartridge Park Chartridge Chesham 01494 791772	18 5270 Parkland	£16 Wd £20 We	No	Restaurant Bars
Farnham Park Park Rd Stoke Poges 01753 643332	18 6172 Parkland	£8 Wd £11 We	No	Full Catering Bars Dress code on course
Iver Hollow Hill Lane Langley Park Rd Iver 01753 655615	9 6214 Parkland		No	Catering Available Golf: Book at Weekend
Little Chalfont Lodge Lane Little Chalfont 01494 764877	9 6800 Parkland	£10 Wd £12 We	No	Full Catering
Princes Risborough Lee Rd Saunderton Lee Princes Risborough 01844 346989	9 5410 Parkland	£10 Wd £12 We (9) £14 Wd £18 We (18)	No	Bar Food Snacks Bar Golf: Book W/e

Name & Address	Holes/Yards Description	Green Fee	Driving Range	Facilities etc.
Silverstone Silverstone Rd Stowe Buckingham 01280 850005	18 6194 Meadowland	£7.50 Wd £12 We	Yes	Full Catering Smart/Casual Dress
Thorney Park Thorney Mill Lane Iver 01895 422095	9 3000 Parkland	£6 Wd £9 We (9) £9 Wd £13 We (18)	No	Restaurant Bar
Three Locks Great Brickhill Milton Keynes 01525 270050	18 5453 Meadowland	£9.50 Wd £11 We	No	Catering Available Bar
Wavendon Golf Centre Lower End Rd Wavendon Milton Keynes 01908 281811	18/5361 9/1424 Par 3 Parkland	£10 Wd £13.50 We	Yes	Carvery Bar Meals Bar
Wexham Park Wexham Street, Wexham Slough 01753 663271	18/5890 9/2851 9/2283	£10 Wd £13.50 We	Yes	Full Catering
Windmill Hill Tattenhoe Lane Bletchley Milton Keynes 01908 648149	18 6773 Parkland		Yes	Catering Available Bar
Wycombe Heights Golf Centre Rayners Avenue Loudwater High Wycombe 01494 816686	18 6253 Parkland	£10.80 Wd £13.90 We	Yes	Restaurant Bar

Name & Address	Holes/Yards Description	Green Fee	Driving Range	Facilities etc.
Abbotsley/Cranwell Eynesbury Hardwicke St Neots 01480 215153	18/6311 18/6087 Parkland/ Meadowland	£25 Wd £30 We £11 Wd £13 We	Yes	Full Catering Bar
Bourn Toft Rd Bourn 01954 718057	18 6273 Parkland	£15 Wd £25 We	No	Restaurant Bar
Cambridge Station Rd Longstanton 01954 789388	9 6908 Parkland	£6 Wd £7.50 We	Yes	Full Catering
Hemingford Abbots Cambridge Rd Hemingford Abbots 01480 495000	9 5468 Parkland	£10 Wd £15 We	Yes	Snacks Bar
Heydon Grange Golf & Country Club Heydon Nr Royston 01763 208988	27 6512/6387/ 6623 Downland/ Parkland	£15	Yes	Restaurants Bars
Kingsway Cambridge Rd Melbourn Nr Royston 01763 262727	9 4910 Meadowland	£6 Wd £7 We	Yes	Bar Snacks
Lakeside Lodge Fen Rd Pidley Huntingdon 01487 740540	18/6821 9 Par3	£9 Wd £15 We	Yes	Full Catering
Old Nene Golf & Country Club Muchwood Lane Bodsey, Ramsey 01487 815622	18 tees 5675 Parkland	£7/£9 (9) Wd/We £10/£14 (18) Wd/We	Yes	Meals Bar Course: Proper golf dress Jeans adm./DrR
Orton Meadows Ham Lane Orton Waterville Peterborough 01733 237478	18 5664 Parkland	£8.50 Wd £11 We	No	
Thorney Golf Centre English Drove Thorney Peterborough 01733 270570	18/6104 9 Par 3	£5.50 Wd £7.50 We	Yes	Restaurant Bar

Name & Address	Holes/Yards Description	Green Fee	Driving Range	Facilities etc.
Thorpe Wood Nene Parkway Peterborough 01733 267701	18 7086 Parkland	£8.80 Wd £11 We	No	
Whaddon Golf Centre Church St Whaddon Nr Royston 01223 207325	9 3795 Parkland	£2.50 Wd £3 We	Yes	Snacks Bar

Name & Address	Holes/Yards Description	Green Fee	Driving Range	Facilities etc.
Adlington Golf Centre Sandy Hey Farm Adlington Macclesfield 01625 850660	9 Par 3 632 Meadowland	£3.50 Wd £4.50 We	Yes	Light Refreshments
Aldersey Green Aldersey Chester 01829 782157	18 6159 Parkland	£12 Wd £15 We	No	Bar Meals Bar Dress Code Applies
Altrincham Stockport Rd Timperley Altrincham 0161 9280761	18 6162 Parkland	£7.15 Wd £9.50 We	Yes	Beefeater Restaurant within grounds
Alvaston Hall Middlewich Rd Nantwich 01270 624341	9 3612 Meadowland	£6	Yes	Full Catering
Antrobus Foggs Lane Antrobus Northwich 01925 730890	18 6220 Meadowland with Lakes	£18 Wd £20 We	Yes	Meals Bar Snacks
Arrowe Park Arrowe Park Woodchurch Birkenhead 0151 6771527	18 6377 Parkland	£6	No	Restaurant
Brackenwood Bracken Lane Bebington Wirral 0151 6083093	18 6285 Parkland	£6	No	
Ellesmere Port Chester Rd Childer Thornton S. Wirral 0151 3397689	18 6432 Parkland/ Meadowland	£5.40 Wd £6.30 We	No	Full Catering
Heyrose Budworth Rd Tabley Knutsford 01565 733664	18 6510 Wooded Meadowland	£19 Wd £24 We	No	Restaurant Bar Golf: Not before 2pm Sat.
Hoylake Carr Lane Hoylake 0151 6322956	18 6313 Parkland		No	Meals & Snacks Bar

Name & Address	Holes/Yards Description	Green Fee	Driving Range	Facilities etc.
Knights Grange Sports Complex, Grange Lane Winsford 01606 552780	9 2995 Meadowland	£2.70 Wd £3.95 We	No	Snacks Hot Drinks
Malkins Bank Betchton Rd Sandbach 01270 765931	18 5971 Parkland	£7.50 Wd £8.50 We	No	Catering Available Bar
Portal Golf & Country Club, Cobblers Cross Tarporley 01829 733933	45 (3 Courses) 7145 Parkland	From £30 £10 (9 Holes)	No	Full Catering
Pryors Hayes Willington Rd Oscroft, Tarvin Nr Chester 01829 741250	18 6074 Parkland	£15 Wd £20 We	No	Full Catering
St Michael Jubilee Dundalk Rd Widnes 0151 4246230	18 5668 Parkland		No	Full Catering Book at weekends
Shrigley Hall Hotel Shrigley Park Pott Shrigley Macclesfield 01625 575757	18 6110 Parkland	£28 Mon/Thu £35 Fri/Sun	No	Full Catering
Styal Station Rd Styal 01625 530063	18 6312 Parkland	£12 Wd £16 We	Yes	Full Catering
Sutton Hall Aston Lane Sutton Weaver Nr Frodsham 01928 714872	18 6547 Parkland		No	
Walton Hall Warrington Rd Higher Walton Warrington 01925 266775	18 6801 Parkland	£6.50 Wd £8 We	No	Full Catering April-October
Westminster Park Hough Green Chester 01244 680231	9 Par 3 900 Links		No	

Name & Address	Holes/Yards Description	Green Fee	Driving Range	Facilities etc.
Bowood Bowood Park Valley Truckle, Camelford 01840 213017	18 6692 Parkland	£20 Wd & We	Yes	Full Catering
Helston Golf & Leisure Wendron Helston 01326 572518	18 2000 (Par3) Park & Downland	£5	No	Bar
Merlin Mawgan Porth Newquay 01637 880257	18 5227 Links type Course	£7 Wd £10 We	Yes	Catering Available
Porthpean St Austell 01726 64613	18 5184 Cliff top / Parkland	£7.50 (9) £12 (18) Wd & We	Yes	Light Lunches Bar
Radnor Golf Centre Radnor Rd Redruth 01209 211059	9 1326 (Par 3) Heathland	£4.80 (9) £7.50 (18) Wd & We	Yes	Bar
St Kew St Kew Highway Nr Wadebridge 01208 841500	9 (18 tees) 4543 Parkland	£8.50 (9) £13 (18)	Yes	Full Catering Bar
Tregenna Castle Hotel St Ives 01736 795254	18 3549 Parkland	£12.50	No	Full Catering Bar
Treloy Newquay 01637 878554	9 2143 Heathland / Parkland	£15 per day	No	
Trethorne Kennards House Launceston 01566 86324	18 6432 Parkland	£17	Yes	Full Catering Bar

Name & Address	Holes/Yards Description	Green Fee	Driving Range	Facilities etc.
Brayton Park Brayton Aspatria, Carlisle 016973 20840	9 2521 Parkland	£5 Wd £6 We	Yes	Full Catering
Dalston Hall Dalston Nr Carlisle 01228 710165	9 5294 Parkland	£5 Wd £6 We	No	Restaurant, Bar Golf: Book tee times W/e & from 4pm
Eden Crosby-on-Eden Carlisle 01228 573003	18 6368 Parkland	£15 Wd £20 We	Yes	Full Catering
Solway Village Golf Centre Solway Village Silloth-on-Solway 016973 31236	9 2000 / Par 3 Parkland		Yes	Restaurant Bar
Stonyholme St Aidans Rd Carlisle 01228 34856	18 5787 Meadowland	£6.50 Wd £8 We	No	Meals

Name & Address	Holes/Yards Description	Green Fee	Driving Range	Facilities etc.
Derby Shakespeare St Sinfin Derby 01332 766462	18 6165 Parkland		No	Catering Available Bar
Grassmoor Golf Centre N. Wingfield Rd Grassmoor Chesterfield 01246 856044	18 5723 Moorland	£7.50 Wd £9 We	Yes	Restaurant Bar
Ilkeston Borough (Pewit) West End Drive Ilkeston 0115 9307704	9 4116 Meadowland	£6 (18 holes)	No	
Maywood Rushy Lane Risley Draycott 0115 9392306	18 6424 Wooded	£15 Wd £20 We	No	Snacks Bar
Tapton Park Murray House Crow Lane Chesterfield 01246 273887	18 6025 Parkland		No	Restaurant Bar

Name & Address	Holes/Yards Description	Green Fee	Driving Range	Facilities etc.
Ashbury Higher Maddaford Southcott Okehampton 01837 55453	18 2000 Par 3 Moorland	£12 Wd £15 We	No	Snacks Bar
Chulmleigh Leigh Rd Chulmleigh 01769 580519	18/1450/ Summer 9/2230 (Winter) Par3 Meadowland	£6.50 Wd & We	No	Light Snacks Bar
Dainton Park Ipplepen Newton Abbot 01803 813812	18 6207 Parkland	£14.50 Wd £17 We	Yes	Full Catering
Dinnaton Dinnaton Sporting & Country Club Ivybridge 01752 892512	9 4089 Parkland	£10 Wd £12.50 We	No	Restaurant Bar
Fingle Glen Family Golf Centre Tedburn St. Mary 01647 61817	9 2483 Parkland	£6 (9) Wd £8.50 (9) We	Yes	Restaurant Bar
Hartland Forest Golf & Leisure Park Tedburn St Mary Nr Exeter 01237 431442	18 6015 Parkland	£15 Wd & We	No	Restaurant Bar
Hele Park Ashburton Rd Newton Abbot 01626 336060	9 5168 Parkland	From £6.50 (9) From £11 (18)	Yes	Restaurant Bar
Highbullen Hotel Chittlehamholt Umberleigh 01769 540561	18 5700 Parkland	£8 Wd & We	No	Full Hotel Facilities
Hurdwick Tavistock Hamlets Tavistock 01822 612746	18 5217 Parkland	£12 Wd & We	No	Snacks Bar
Libbaton High Bickington Umberleigh 01769 560269	18 6494 Parkland	£14 Wd £16 We	Yes	Catering Available
Mortehoe & Woolacombe Easewell, Mortehoe 01271 870225	9 4638 Parkland /Seaside	£6 (9) £10 (18) Wd & We	No	Full Catering

Name & Address	Holes/Yards Description	Green Fee	Driving Range	Facilities etc.
Northbrook Topsham Rd Exeter 01392 57436	18 1078 Wooded Parkland	£2 Wd & We	No	Vending Machines
Sparkwell Welbeck Manor Hotel Sparkwell Plymouth 01752 837219	9 5772 Parkland	£5 (9) Wd £6 (9) We	No	Full Catering Bar (Hotel)
Waterbridge Down St Mary Nr Crediton 01363 85111	9 3908 Parkland	£5 (9) Wd £6.50 (9) We	No	Light Snacks unless ordered

Name & Address	Holes/Yards Description	Green Fee	Driving Range	Facilities etc.
Bulbury Club Bulbury Lane Lytchett Matravers Nr. Poole, 01929 459574	18 6300 Parkland	£18 Wd £20 We	No	Full Catering Bar
Canford Magna Knighton Lane Canford Magna Wimborne 01202 593901	18/6200 18/6300 Parkland	£14.50 Wd £18 We	Yes	Full Catering
Chedington Court South Perrott Beaminster 01935 981413	18 9/6754 Parkland	£15 Wd £18 We £10 We £12 We	No	Refreshments available
Crane Valley West Farm Romford, Verwood 01202 814088	9 2060 Woodland	£5.50 Wd £6.50 We	Yes	Full Catering Bar Proper golfing attire
Dorset Heights Belchallwell Okeford Fitzpaine Blandford Forum 01258 861386	18 6162 Parkland	£12 Wd £17 We	No	Lunches, Tea Evening Meals
Dudmoor Farm Dudmoor Farm Rd Christchurch 01202 483980	9 1428m Woodland	£4.50 (18 holes)	No	Snacks Soft drinks
Ferndown Forest Forest Links Rd Ferndown 01202 876096	18 4621 Parkland	£12 Wd £15 We	Yes	Snack Bar Restaurant Bars
Folke Golf Centre Alweston Sherborne 01963 23330	9 (18 tees) 5430 Parkland	£4/£7 Wd £5/£9 We	Yes	Snacks Bar
Iford Bridge Sports Centre Barrack Rd, Iford Christchurch 01202 473817	9 4290 Parkland/ Meadowland	£5.70 Wd £6.45 We	Yes	Snacks Bar
Lyons Gate Lyons Gate Farm Dorchester 01300 345239	9 3838 Wooded Farmland	£4.50 (9) Wd £5 (9) We	No	Light Refreshments
Parley Parley Green Lane Hurn, Christchurch 01202 591600	9 4584 Parkland	£4.50/ £5.50 (9) £7/£8.50 (18)	Yes	Snacks Restaurant Bar

Name & Address	Holes/Yards Description	Green Fee	Driving Range	Facilities etc.
Queen's Park Queen's Park West Drive, Bournemouth 01202 302611	18 6319 Parkland	£12	No	Restaurant Bar
Riversmeet Leisure Centre Stoney Lane South Christchurch 01202 477987	18 1455 Seaside	£4.20 Adult £2.50 OAP & Jnr	No	Restaurant Bar
Rushmore Park Tollard Royal Shaftesbury 01725 516326			No	
Solent Meads Par 3 Rolls Drive Nr. Hengistbury Head Bournemouth 01202 420795	18 2235 Seaside	£4	Yes	Light Refreshments
Sturminster Marshall Moor Lane Sturminster Marshall Nr Blandford Forum 01258 858444	9 4882 Parkland	£7 (9 holes) £10 (18)	No	Restaurant Bar
Wessex Golf Centre Radipole Lane Weymouth 01305 784737	9 Par 3	£3.85	Yes	
Wolfedale Charminster Nr. Dorchester 01305 260186	15 4332 Meadowland	£7 Wd £10 We	No	Refreshments

Name & Address	Holes/Yards Description	Green Fee	Driving Range	Facilities etc.
Hall Garth Golf & Country Club Coatham Mundeville Nr Darlington 01325 300400	9 6621 Parkland	£10 Wd £12.50 We	No	Catering Available Bar
Hobson Municipal Burnopfield Nr. Consett 01207 271069	18 6403 Parkland	£12 Wd £15 We Summer	No	Restaurant Bar Special Twilight & Winter Rates
Norton Junction Rd Stockton-on-Tees 01642 676385	18 5855 Parkland	£9 Wd £10 We	No	Correct shoes No Jeans Half set clubs each
Oak Leaf (Aycliffe) School Aycliffe Lane Newton Aycliffe 01325 310820	18 5334 Parkland	£6 Wd £7 We	Yes	Catering at sports complex
Ramside Ramside Hall Carrville Durham 0191 3865282	27 holes Parkland		No	Full Catering
Ryhope c/o Winfield 30 Rosslyn Avenue Ryhope Sunderland 0191 5237333	9 4601 Parkland	£6	No	Full Catering
Stressholme Golf Centre Snipe Lane Darlington 01352 461002	18 6432 Parkland	£8.40 Wd £10 We	No	Catering Available Bar

Name & Address	Holes/Yards Description	Green Fee	Driving Range	Facilities etc.
Basildon Clay Hill Lane Basildon 01268 533297	18 6236 Parkland	£9 Wd £15 We	No	Full Catering
Belfairs Park Starter's Hut Eastwood Rd North Leigh-on-Sea 01702 525345	18 5795 Parkland/ Wooded	£8.50 Wd £13 We	No	Restaurant
Belhus Park (Thurrock) Belhus Park South Ockendon 01708 854260	18 5527 Parkland	£8 Wd £12 We	Yes	Restaurant Bar
Benton Hall Wickham Hill Witham 01376 502454	9 Par 3 Parkland	£16 Wd £20 We	Yes	Restaurant Bar
Bunsay Downs Little Baddow Rd Woodham Walter Nr Maldon 01245 222648	9/2932 9 Par 3 Meadowland	£10 Wd £11 We £8/Par 3	Yes	Catering Available
Castle Point Somnes Avenue Canvey Island 01268 510830	18 6176 Seaside Links	£8.10 Wd £12.20 We	Yes	Restaurant Bar
Earls Colne Golf & Country Club Earls Colne Nr Colchester 01787 224466	9 1520 Meadowland	£16 Wd £20 WE	Yes	Full Catering
Fairlop Waters Forest Rd Barkingside Ilford 0181 5009911	18/6281 9/1167 Par 3 Heathland	£7.75 Wd £11.25 We	Yes	Daltons American Diner Bar
Hartswood King George's Playing Fields, Ingrave Rd Brentwood 01277 218850	18 6160 Parkland	£8 Wd £12 We	No	Catering Available by Arrangement
High Beech Wellington Hill Loughton 0181 5087323	9/847 Par 3 9/1477 Par 3 Parkland	£2.80 Wd & We £3.25 Wd £4.25 We	No	Snacks

Name & Address	Holes/Yards Description	Green Fee	Driving Range	Facilities etc.
Langdon Hills Lower Dunton Rd Bulphan 01268 548444	9 Parkland	£6 (18 holes) Wd £7.50 (18 holes) We	Yes	Restaurant Bars
Loughton Clay's Lane Loughton 0181 5022923	9 4652 Parkland	£5.50Wd/9 £6.50We/9 £8 Wd/18 £10 We/18	No	Bar Snacks
North Weald Village Par 3 Epping Rd (B181) North Weald 01992 524142				
Pipps Hill (Leisure Complex) Cranes Farm Rd Basildon 01268 271571	9 2829 Meadowland	£5.50/9 holes £9.50/18 holes	Yes	Full Catering
Risebridge (Havering) Lower Bedfords Rd Romford 01708 741429	18 5310 Parkland	£9.20 Wd £11.20 We	No	Snacks
Towerlands Panfield Rd Braintree 01376 347951	9 5406 Meadowland	After 12.30 We	Yes	Restaurant Bar

Name & Address	Holes/Yards Description	Green Fee	Driving Range	Facilities etc.
Brickhampton Court Cheltenham Rd Churchdown 01452 859444	18/6387 9/1859 Parkland	£16 Wd £22.50 We £6.50/£8 (9 hole)	Yes Floodlit	Full Catering Bar Correct Golfing Dress
Canons Court Bradley Green Wotton-under-Edge 01453 843128	9 5323 Meadowland	£8 Wd £10 We	No	Full Catering Bar
Forest Hills Mile End Rd Coleford 01594 562899	18 5674 Parkland	£10 Wd £13 We	Yes	Full Catering
Naunton Downs Naunton Cheltenham 01451 850090	18 6078 Downland	£19.95/day	No	Restaurant Bar
Pickrup Hall Hotel Pickrup Tewkesbury 01684 296200	18 6431 Parkland	£22 Wd £25 We Summer Prices	No	Full Catering
Sherdons Manor Farm Tredington Tewkesbury 01684 274782	9 2654 Parkland	£6 Wd (9) £7.50 We £10 Wd (18) £13 We	Yes	Limited Catering
Thornbury Golf Centre Bristol Rd Thornbury 01454 281144	18/6154 18/2800 Par 3 Parkland	£14 Wd £16 We	Yes	Full Catering Lodge: 11 Rooms

Name & Address	Holes/Yards Description	Green Fee	Driving Range	Facilities etc.
Basingstoke Golf Centre, Worting Rd West Ham, Basingstoke 01256 350054	9 908 par 3 Parkland	£2.60 Wd £3 We	Yes	
Bishopswood Bishopswood Lane Tadley, Basingstoke 0118 981 5213	9 6474 Parkland	£9 (9) £14 (18) Wd	Yes	Restaurant Bar
Blacknest Binstead Rd, Binstead Alton 01420 22888	18 5858 Parkland	£14.50 Wd £16.50 We	Yes	Restaurant Bar
Blackwater Valley Fox Lane Eversley Cross Basingstoke 01252 874725	9 4744 Parkland	£8 (9) Wd £10 (9) We	No	Full Catering
Chilworth Golf Centre Main Rd Chilworth Southampton 01703 740544	18 5740 Parkland	£12 Wd £15 We	Yes	Full Facilities
Dean Farm Main Rd, Kingsley Bordon 01420 472313	9 1797 Parkland	£4 (9) £6.50 (18) Wd & We	No	Snacks Bar
Dibden Main Rd, Dibden Southampton 01703 207508	18 5986 Parkland	£7.25 Wd £10 We	Yes	Full Catering
Furzeley Furzeley Rd Denmead 01705 231180	18 4247 Parkland	£9.80 Wd £11.50 We £5.30/ £6.30 (9)	No	Restaurant
Great Salterns Portsmouth Golf Centre, Burrfields Rd Portsmouth 01705 664549	18 5737 Seaside/ Parkland	£11.50 Wd & We	Yes	Full Catering at adjoining pub
Moors Valley Golf Centre, Country Park Horton Rd Ashley Heath Nr Ringwood 01425 479776	18 6270 Parkland/ Heathland	£5 (11) Wd £6 (11) We	Yes	Catering Facilities Bar

Name & Address	Holes/Yards Description	Green Fee	Driving Range	Facilities etc.
Old Thorns Longmoor Rd Griggs Green Liphook 01428 724555	18 6533 Parkland	£35 Wd £45 We	Yes	Full Catering Dress Restrictions
Otterbourne Poles Lane Otterbourne Nr Winchester 01962 775225	9 1939	£3.50 Wd £4.50 We	No	Snacks
Paultons Golf Centre Old Salisbury Rd Ower Nr Romsey 01703 81334	18/6238 9 Par 3 Parkland	£15 (18) Wd £18 We	Yes	Restaurant Bars
Southampton Golf Course Rd Bassett, Southampton 01703 767996	18 / 6213 9 / 2385 Parkland	£8.60 Wd £11.90 We	No	Sacks Bar
Southwood Ively Rd, Cove Farnborough 01252 548700	18 5738 Parkland	£11.50 Wd £14 We	No	Snacks Bar
Wellow Ryedown Lane East Wellow Romsey 01749 322872	3 x 9 5966, 6320, 5844 Parkland	£16 Wd £19 We	No	Full Catering Normal Dress Code Golf Shoes must be worn
Westridge Brading Rd, Ryde Isle of Wight 01983 613131	9 3228	£7 (9) Wd £8 (9) We	Yes	Snacks Bar Changing Rms. Showers
Wickham Park Titchfield Lane Wickham Nr Fareham 01329 833342	18 6022 Parkland	£8 Wd £11 We	No	Snacks No jeans
Worldham Park Caker Lane East Worldham Nr Alton 01420 543151	18 5836 Parkland	£11 Wd £13 We	Yes	Full Catering Bar No jeans

Name & Address	Holes/Yards Description	Green Fee	Driving Range	Facilities etc.
Belmont Lodge & Golf Course Belmont House Hereford 01432 352666	18 6511 Parkland/ River Meadows	£12/17 Wd £18/25 We	No	Restaurant Snacks Bar all day Normal Golfing Dress
Burghill Valley Tillington Rd Burghill Hereford 01432 760456	18 6239 Parkland		No	Light Meals Bar
Grove Golf Centre Fordbridge Leominster 01568 610602	9 3560 Parkland	£4 Wd £5 We	Yes	Snacks Bar Clubhouse Summer '98
Hereford Municipal Hereford Leisure Centre Holmer Rd Hereford 01432 278178	9 3060 Meadowland	£3.60 Wd £4.95 We	No	Restaurant Bar

Name & Address	Holes/Yards Description	Green Fee	Driving Range	Facilities etc.
Abbey View Holywell Hill Westminster Lodge St Albans 01727 868227	9 1440 Parkland	£4.75 Adult £2.50 Junior Wd & We	No	Catering Available
Aldwickbury Park Piggotshill Lane Harpenden 01582 760112	18/6352 9/1000 Par 3		No	Restaurant Bars
Batchwood Centre Batchwood Drive St Albans 01727 844250	18 6487 Parkland	£8 Wd £10.50 We	No	Restaurant Bar
Cheshunt Park Lane, Cheshunt 01992 624009	18 6613 Parkland	£10 Wd £13.50 We	No	Cafeteria Bookings at Weekend
Family Golf Centre Jack's Hill Graveley 01462 482929	18/6646 9/975 Par 3 Links/ Downland	£14.75 Wd £21 We/18 £3.50 Wd £4.50 We/9	Yes	Restaurant Bar Coffee Shop
The Hertfordshire Broxbournebury Man. White Stubbs Lane Broxbourne 01992 466666	18 6410 Parkland	£21 Wd £25 We £33/£39/ Day	Yes	Restaurant Bar
Little Hay Golf Comp. Box Lane, Bovingdon Hemel Hempstead 01442 833798	18 6678 9 hole Pitch & Putt/Parkland	£10 Wd £14.25 We (18)	Yes	Full Catering
Mill Green Gypsy Lane Welwyn Garden City 01707 276900	18/6615 9 Par 3 Parkland/ Woodland	£27.50 Wd £32.50 We	No	Restaurant Snacks Bar
Panshanger Old Herns Lane Welwyn Garden City 01707 333350	18 6347 Parkland	£10.50 Wd £12.50 We	No	Lunches
Rickmansworth Moor Lane Rickmansworth 01923 775278	18 4469 Parkland	£8.50 Wd £12 We	No	Catering Bar
Stevenage Aston Lane, Aston Stevenage 01438 880424	18 6341 Parkland/ Meadowland	£8.80 Wd £10.80 We	No	Full Catering Bar
Tudor Park Sports Ground Clifford Rd New Barnet 0181 4490282	9 1836 Parkland		No	

Name & Address	Holes/Yards Description	Green Fee	Driving Range	Facilities etc.
Birchwood Park Wilmington Dartford 01322 660554	18 6364 Meadowland	£14 Wd £23 We	Yes	Full Catering
Boughton Golf Brickfield Lane Boughton Nr Faversham 01227 752277	18 6452 Upland	£15 Wd £20 We	Yes	Restaurant Bar
Cobtree Manor Park Chatham Rd Maidstone 01622 753276	18 5586 Parkland	£11 Wd £16 We	No	Catering Available
Darenth Valley Station Rd Shoreham 01959 522944	18 6327 Meadowland	£12 Wd £16 We	No	Bar Meals Society Catering
Deangate Ridge Hoo Rochester 01634 251180	18 6300 Parkland	£9.60 (18) Wd £12.70 (18) We	No	Lunch & Dinner Served
Hewitts Golf Centre Court Rd Orpington 01689 896266	18/6077 9/Par 3 Parkland	£15 Wd(18) £4 Wd(9)	Yes	Restaurant Bar Society Catering No denim jeans
High Elms High Elms Rd Downe 01689 858175	18 6210 Parkland	£9.50 Wd £12.50 We	No	Full Catering
Hilden Golf Centre Rings Hill Hildenborough 01732 833607	9 1558	£5.75 Wd £7.25 We	Yes	Full Catering
Homelands Bettergolf Centre, Ashford Rd Kingsnorth Nr Ashford 01233 661620	9 2205 Parkland	£7 Wd (9) £8 We (9)	Yes	Snacks Bar
Jack Nicklaus Golf Centre Sidcup By-Pass Chislehurst 0181 3081610	9 Par 3 1055	£5 Wd £6 We	No	Full Catering
Leeds Castle Leeds Castle Maidstone 01622 880467	9 2880 Parkland	£8.50 Wd £9.50 We	No	Snacks No denim jeans

Name & Address	Holes/Yards Description	Green Fee	Driving Range	Facilities etc.
Lullingstone Park Park Gate Chelsfield Orpington 01959 533793	18 6068 Parkland	£9 Wd £11 We Summer	No	Snacks Bar
Lydd Romney Rd Lydd Romney Marsh 01797 320808	18 6517 Links	£16 Wd £20 We	No	Restaurant Bar
North Foreland Convent Rd Broadstairs 01843 862140	18 1752 Seaside/ Clifftop	£5.50 Wd & We	No	Catering Available
Oastpark Malling Rd Snodland 01634 242661	18 6173 Parkland	£8.50 Wd £12 We	No	Restaurant Bar Proper Dress
Park Wood Chestnut Avenue Westerham 01959 577744	18 6835 Parkland & Lakes	£20 Wd £30 We	No	Restaurant Bar
Poult Wood Higham Lane Tonbridge 01732 364039	18 5569 9/1281 Wooded	£11/£16 (18)Wd/We £4.90/ £6.20 (9)	No	Restaurant Bar Societies Welcome
Romney Warren St Andrews Rd Littlestone New Romney 01679 363355	18 5126 Links	£10 Wd £15 We	No	Restaurant Bar
Upchurch River Valley Oak Lane Upchurch Sittingbourne 01634 360626	18 6237 Moorland/ Seaside	£10.45 Wd £13.45 We	Yes	Restaurant Bars
Weald of Kent Maidstone Rd Headcorn 01622 890866	18 6240 Parkland	£16.50 Wd £18.50 We	No	Full Catering

Name & Address	Holes/Yards Description	Green Fee	Driving Range	Facilities etc.
Allerton Allerton Liverpool 18 0151 4281046	18/5494 9/1847 Parkland	£6.50/ £7.50 (18) £3.90/ £4.40 (9)	No	Catering by arrangement Golf: Book for 18 hole course
Beacon Park Beacon Lane, Dalton Up Holland Wigan 01695 622700	18 5996 Parkland		Yes	Bar Meals Bar
Bootle Dunnings Bridge Rd Bootle, Merseyside 0151 9286196	18 6362 Seaside	£4.80 Wd £6.40 We	No	Meals
Bowring Bowring Park Roby Rd, Huyton Liverpool 0151 4891901	18 5620 Parkland	£4.55 per round	No	Snacks
Duxbury Park Duxbury Park Chorley 01257 241378	18 6270 Parkland		No	Catering Available
Golf Centre Wigan Rd Westhoughton Nr Bolton	18 6400 Parkland	£6.50 Wd £10 We	No	Catering Available
Haigh Hall Haigh Country Park Aspull Wigan 01942 833337	18 6423 Parkland	£5.95 Wd £8.50 We	No	Cafeteria
Heaton Park Prestwich Manchester 0161 7980295	18 5766 Parkland	£6.50 Wd £7.50 We	No	
Liverpool (Kirkby) Ingoe Lane Kirkby Liverpool 32 0151 5465435	18 6706 Meadowland	£6.20	No	Cafeteria Bar
Pennington Pennington Country Park, St Helen's Rd Leigh, Gtr Manchester 01942 682852	9 2919 Parkland	£3.25 Wd £4.50 We	No	Snack Bar

Name & Address	Holes/Yards Description	Green Fee	Driving Range	Facilities etc.
Poulton-le-Fylde Myrtle Farm Breck Rd Poulton-le-Fylde 01253 892444	9 6056 Meadowland	£5.50 Wd £7.50 We	No	Snacks Lunches Bar
Regent Park (Bolton) Links Rd Lostock, Bolton 01204 844170	18 6130 Parkland	£6 Wd £8 We	No	Restaurant Take-away Bar
Sherdley Park Sherdley Park St Helen's, Merseyside 01744 815518	18 5974 Parkland	£6.20 Wd £7.20 We	No	Cafeteria Bar
Southport Municipal Park Rd West Southport 01704 535286	18 6139 Seaside	£5.50 Wd £7.50 We	No	Catering Available
Standish Court Rectory Lane Standish, Wigan 01257 425777	18 5609 Parkland	£12.50 Wd £15 We	No	Catering Available Golf: Phone for tee times
Towneley Todmorden Rd Burnley 01282 38473	18 5811 Parkland	£7 Wd £8 We	No	Restaurant Bar Golf: Normal Dress Rules
William Wroe Pennybridge Lane Flixton Manchester 0161 7488680	18 4395 Parkland	£6.30 Wd £8.40 We	No	

Name & Address	Holes/Yards Description	Green Fee	Driving Range	Facilities etc.
Beedles Lake Broome Lane East Goscote 0116 2606759	18 6573 Parkland	£6 Wd £8 We	Yes	Full Catering
Blaby Lutterworth Rd Blaby 0116 2784804	9 5132	£4 Wd £6 We	Yes	Bar Meals Bar
Enderby Mill Lane Enderby 0116 2849388	9 4232 Heathland	£4.50 Wd £5.50 We	No	Bar Snacks Bar
Forest Hill Markfield Lane Botcheston 01455 824800	18 6111 Parkland	£10 Wd £15 We	Yes	Restaurant Bar
Greetham Valley Wood Lane Greetham Nr Oakham 01780 460004	27 5875/6362 9 Par 3	£20 Wd £24 We £3.50 Wd £4 We	Yes	Restaurant Snacks Bar
Humberstone Heights Gipsy Lane Leicester 0116 2761905	18 6343 Parkland	£6.80 Wd £7.95 We	Yes	Snacks Bar Meals by Arrangement
Langton Hall Langton Hall Leicester 01858 545134	9 6742 Parkland	£9 Wd £9 We	No	Light Snacks Bar
Shelthorpe Poplar Rd Loughborough 01509 267766	18 2080 Par 3 Parkland	£2.85	No	
Stoke Albany Ashley Rd Stoke Albany Market Harborough 01858 535208	18 6132 Parkland	£12 Wd £16 We	Practice Area	Restaurant Bar Snacks Bar
Western Park Scudamore Rd Braunstone Frith Leicester 0116 2872339	18 6518 Parkland	£4.95 Wd £5.95 We	No	Catering Available

Name & Address	Holes/Yards Description	Green Fee	Driving Range	Facilities etc.
Belton Woods Hotel & Country Club Belton Nr Grantham 01476 593200	18/6808 18/6834 9/1184 Par 3 Parkland	£20 (18) £2.50 (9)	Yes	Full Catering Bar
Boston West Hubbert's Bridge Boston 01205 290540	9 6346 Lowland	£5.50 Wd £6.50 We	Yes	Full Catering Bar Golf Academy
Forest Pines Briggate Lodge Inn Ermine St Nr Brigg 01652 650770	27 holes 9/6882 9/6694 9/6394 Forest	£30 Round £35 Day Ticket Wd/We	Yes	Full Catering
Gedney Hill West Drove Gedney Hill Nr Holbeach 01406 330922	18 5357 Links	£5.75 Wd £8.75 We	Yes	Restaurant Bar Smart Dress
Grange Park Butterwick Rd Messingham Scunthorpe 01724 762945	13/4122 9 Par 3 Parkland	£5.50 Wd £7.50 We Par 3 £2.50 Wd £3.50 We	Yes	Coffee Bar
Hirst Priory Hirst Priory Park Crowle Nr Scunthorpe 01724 711621	18 6119 Parkland	£11.75 Wd £14.50 We	No	Full Catering
Horncastle West Ashby Horncastle 01507 526800	18 5717 Heathland	£10 Wd & We	Yes	Full Catering
Kingsway Kingsway Scunthorpe 01724 840945	9 1915 Parkland	£2.95 Wd £3.45 We	No	Snacks
Kirton Holme Holme Rd Nr Boston 01205 290669	9 2884 Parkland	£4.40 Wd £5.50 We	No	Snacks Bar Meals Bar
Market Rasen Race Course Legsby Rd Market Rasen 01673 843434	9 2377	£4 Wd £5 We	No	Catering Available

Name & Address	Holes/Yards Description	Green Fee	Driving Range	Facilities etc.
Martin Moor Blankney Rd Martin Moor Metheringham 01526 378243	9 3357 Parkland	£4 Wd £5 We	No	Bar Buffet by Arrangement
Millfield Laughterton Torksey Nr Lincoln 01427 718473	18/5986 15/4100 9/1500 Par 3	£7 (18) £4 (9)	Yes	Light Refreshments
Pottergate Moor Lane Branston Nr Lincoln 01522 794867	9 2519 Mature Parkland	£6 (9) £8 (18)	No	Snacks Bar Smart Simulator/ All Weather Golf
South Kyme Skinners Lane South Kyme Lincoln 01526 861113	18 6597 Fenland	£10 Wd £12 We	No	Catering Available Bar
Southview Leisure Park Burgh Rd Skegness 01754 760589	9 2408 Parkland	£6 (18 holes)	No	Full Catering
Sudbrook Moor Carlton Scroop Nr Grantham 01400 250796	9 4566 Parkland	£5 per day/Wd £7 per day/We	No	Coffee Shop
Swingtime (Grimsby) Cromwell Rd Grimsby 01472 250555	9 2426 Parkland	£6 Wd £7 We	Yes	Limited Catering

Name & Address	Holes/Yards Description	Green Fee	Driving Range	Facilities etc.
Brent Valley Church Rd Hanwell 01268 793625	18 5440 Meadowland	£8.70 Wd £12.95 We	No	Restaurant
Chingford Bury Rd Chingford 0181 5292195	18 6400 Parkland	£9 Wd £12.50 We	No	Snacks Red outer garment to be worn
Lee Valley Leisure Golf Course Picketts Lock Lane Edmonton 0181 8033611	18 4902 Parkland	£10 Wd £13 We	Yes	Snacks Bar
Richmond Park Roehampton Gate Richmond Park 0181 8763205	18/5909 18/6100 Parkland	£9.25 Wd £13 We	Yes	Cafe Golf Shoes Book at We
Riverside Summerton Way Thamesmead 0181 3107975	9 5482 Reclaimed Marshland	£5 Wd £6.50 We	Yes	a la carte Catering Bars
Trent Park Bramley Rd Oakwood 0181 3667432	18 6085 Parkland	£11 Wd £14 We	Yes (Heated)	Restaurant Snacks / Bar Buggies (Summer)

Name & Address	Holes/Yards Description	Green Fee	Driving Range	Facilities etc.
Douglas Pulrose Rd Douglas 01624 675952	18 5922 Parkland		No	Meals May/Sept by Arrangement
Mount Murray Santon 01624 661111	18 6709 Parkland	£18 Wd £24 We	Yes	Restaurant Bistro
Port St Mary Golf Pavilion Port St Mary 01624 834932	9 5418 Seaside links	£12 Wd £14 We	No	Restaurant Cafeteria Bar

Name & Address	Holes/Yards Description	Green Fee	Driving Range	Facilities etc.
Airlinks Southall Lane Hounslow 0181 5611418	18 6001 Meadowland/ Parkland	£10.75 Wd £13.50 We	Yes	Catering Available Bar
Edgewarebury Edgeware Way Edgeware 0181 9583571	9 1045 Par 3	£4	No	
Harefield Place The Drive Harefield Place Uxbridge 01895 231169	18 5711 Parkland	£10 Wd £15 We	No	Full Catering
Harrow Hill Kenton Rd Harrow 0181 8643754	9 Par 3 950 Parkland	£3.80	No	Soft Drinks
Haste Hill The Drive Northwood 01923 826078	18 5787 Parkland	£10 Wd £15 We	No	Catering Available
Hazelwood Croysdale Avenue Sunbury-on-Thames 01932 770981	9 5660 Parkland	£7 Wd £8.50We	Yes	Restaurant Bar Seminar Room
Horsenden Hill Woodland Rise Greenford 0181 9024555	9 3264 Parkland	£4.40 Wd £6.50 We	No	Restaurant Bar
Hounslow Heath Staines Rd Hounslow 0181 570 5271	18 5901 Parkland	£7.50 Wd £10.50 We	No	Snacks Soft Drinks
London Golf Centre Ruislip Rd Northolt 0181 8453180	9 (18 tees) 5836 Parkland	£6 (9)Wd £7.50 (9) We	Yes	Bistro Bars
Perivale Park Stockdove Way Argyle Rd Greenford 0181 5757116	9 2648 Parkland	£4.40 Wd £6.50 We	No	Cafeteria
Ruislip Ickenham Rd Ruislip 01895 638835	18 5702 Parkland	£10 Wd £15 We	Yes	Catering Available

Name & Address	Holes/Yards Description	Green Fee	Driving Range	Facilities etc.
Sunbury Charlton Lane Shepperton 01932 772898	18 6210 Parkland	£10 Wd £12 We	Yes	Catering Available
Twickenham Park Staines Rd Twickenham 0181 7831698	9 3109 Parkland	£6 Wd £7 We	Yes	Snacks Bar
Whitewebbs Beggars Hollow Clay Hill Enfield 0181 3632951	18 5800 Parkland	£10.60 Wd £12.60 We	No	Cafe

Name & Address	Holes/Yards Description	Green Fee	Driving Range	Facilities etc.
Caldecott Hall Beccles Rd Fritton Great Yarmouth 01493 488488	9/6842 9 Par 3	£15 (18 holes) Wd £20 (18 holes) We	No	Snacks Bar (200 yds)
Dunham Little Dunham Nr Swaffam King's Lynn 01328 701728	9 4964 Parkland	£9 Wd £12 We	No	Snacks Bar
Dunston Hall Ipswich Rd Norwich 01508 470178	10 (18 tees) 6053 Meadowland	£15 Wd £18 We	Yes	Full Catering
Eagles 39 School Rd Tilney All-Saints King's Lynn 01553 827147	9/4284 9 Par 3 Moorland	£6 Wd £7 We	Yes	Bar
Fakenham Sports Centre The Race Course Fakenham 01328 862867	9 5992 Parkland	£14 Wd £18 We (pm only)	No	Catering in Sports Centre
Links Country Park West Runton 01263 837691	9 2421 Downland	£20 Wd £25 We £15/£20 (Winter) All per day	No	Full Catering Free Golf/hotel residents 1/2 Price twilight round
Mattishall South Green Mattishall Dereham 01362 850111	9 2953 Parkland		No	
Sprowston Park Wroxham Rd Sprowston Norwich 01603 410657	18 5985 Parkland	£12 Wd £15 We	Yes	Full Catering
Wensum Valley Beech Avenue Taverham Norwich 01603 261012	18/6000 9/2953 Parkland	£12 Wd £15 We	Yes	Full Catering

Name & Address	Holes/Yards Description	Green Fee	Driving Range	Facilities etc.
Brampton Heath Sandy Lane Church Brampton 01604 843939	18 6233 Parkland/ Meadowland	£12 Wd £16 We	Yes	Full Catering
Corby Stamford Rd Weldon 01536 260756	18 6677 Parkland	£7 Wd £9 We	No	Meals Snacks
Delapre Park Eagle Drive Nene Valley Way Northampton 01604 764036	18/6269 9/2109	£7.30 Wd £9.50 We	Yes	Full Catering
Farthingstone Hotel Golf/Leisure Complex Farthingstone Towcester 01327 361291	18 6300 Parkland	£10 Wd £15 We	No	Full Catering
Kingfisher Lakes Buckingham Rd Deanshanger 01908 562332	9 2600 Parkland	£5 /9 holes £10 /18 holes	Yes	Full Catering

Name & Address	Holes/Yards Description	Green Fee	Driving Range	Facilities etc.
Bedlingtonshire Acorn Bank Bedlington 01670 822457	18 6813 Meadowland/ Parkland	£15 Wd £20 We	No	Full Catering
Belford South Rd Belford 01668 213433	9 6304 Parkland	£9 Wd £10 We	Yes	Snacks Bar Meals Bar
Burgham Park Near Felton Morpeth 01670 787898	18 6751 Parkland		No	Full Catering Bar
Matfen Hall Matfen 01661 886500	18/6744 9/ Par 3	£19 Wd £23 We	Yes	Full Catering Bar
Swarland Hall Coast View Swarland Morpeth 01670 787010	18 6628 Parkland	£14 Wd £18 We	No	Bar Meals Bar
Tynedale Tyne Green Hexham 01434 608154	9 5403 Parkland		No	Full Catering
Wallsend Bigges Main Wallsend-on-Tyne 0191 2621973	18 6608 Parkland	£11 Wd £13.50 We	Yes	Hot & Cold Snacks

Name & Address	Holes/Yards Description	Green Fee	Driving Range	Facilities etc.
Bondhay Golf & Fishing Club Bondhay Lane Whitwell, Worksop 01909 723608	18/6800 9/Family Parkland	£20 Wd £25 We / (18) £4 (9)	Yes	Full Catering / All day & Evening
Bramcote Hills Thoresby Rd (off Derby Rd) Bramcote, Nottingham 0115 9281880	18 Par 3 1501 Parkland	£5.40 Wd £5.90We	No	Refreshments
Edwalton Edwalton Village Nottingham 0115 9234775	9/3336 9 Par 3/ 1563	£4.40 (Main) £2.50 (Par 3)	No	Lunches Bar Snacks Bar
Kilton Forest Blyth Rd Worksop 01909 472488	18 6444 Parkland	£7 Wd £8.25 We	No	Bar Meals Bar
Leen Valley Golf Centre Wigwam Lane Hucknall 0115 9642037	18 6233 Parkland	£8.50 Wd £9.50 We	No	Full Catering
Nottingham City Lawton Drive Bulwell Nottingham 0115 9278021	18 6128 Parkland	£10	No	Catering Bar Dress rules in Clubhouse
Ramsdale Park Golf Centre Oxton Rd Calverton 0115 9655600	18/6546 18/2844 Par 3 Parkland	£14/£15.50 (18) £7.50 Par 3 (18)	Yes	Full Catering
Trent Lock Golf Centre Lock Lane Sawley Long Eaton 0115 9464398	18 6211 Parkland	£10	Yes	Restaurant Bar

Name & Address	Holes/Yards Description	Green Fee	Driving Range	Facilities etc.
Banbury Aynho Rd Adderbury Banbury 01295 810419	18 6365 Parkland	£8 Wd £10 We	No	Catering by Arrangement Undergoing Alterations
Brailes Sutton Lane Brailes, Banbury 01608 685336	18 6270 Parkland	£13 Wd £15 We	No	Full Catering
Carswell Golf & Country Club Carswell Nr Faringdon 01367 870422	18 6133 Parkland	£13 Wd £18 We	Yes	Catering Available Golf Shoes No jeans/t'suits
Chesterton Chesterton Bicester 01869 242023	18 6229 Meadowland	£12 Wd £15 We	No	Full Catering by Arrangement Book golf ahead
Drayton Park Steventon Rd Drayton 01235 550607	18 5503 Parkland	£12 Wd £15 We	Yes	Meals, Bar Golf Shoes No jeans/ tracksuits
Hadden Hill Wallingford Rd (A4130) Didcot 01235 510410	18 6563 Parkland	£12 Wd £16 We	Yes	Restaurant Bar Advisable to book golf No jeans
Kirtlington Kirtlington 01869 351133	18 5100 metres	£12 Wd £18 We	Yes	Catering Available
Lyneham Chipping Norton 01993 831841	18 6669 Parkland	£15 Wd £18 We	Yes	Catering Book ahead Golf Shoes. No jeans/track suits
Rye Hill Milcombe Banbury 01295 721818	18 6692 Links Style	£10 Wd £12 We	No	Full Catering
Studley Wood The Straight Mile Horton-cum-Studley 01865 351144	18 6711 Woodland	£18 Wd £25 We	Yes	Restaurant
Waterstock Thame Rd Waterstock, Oxford 01844 338093	18/6482 9 (under construction) Parkland	£13 Wd £16.50 We	Yes Floodlit	Full Catering
Witney Downs Rd Witney 01993 779000	18 6675	£13 Wd £18 We	Yes	Restaurant Book Golf Ahead

Name & Address	Holes/Yards Description	Green Fee	Driving Range	Facilities etc.
Aqualate Stafford Rd Newport 01952 811699	9 5963 Parkland	£5 Wd £7 We	Yes	Light Refreshments
Cadmore Lodge Berrington Green Tenbury Wells 01584 810044	9 5129 Parkland	£7 Wd £10 We	No	Full Catering
Chesterton Valley Chesterton Nr Worfield Bridgnorth 01746 783682	9 3129 Meadowland	£6.50	No	Telephone first
Cleobury Mortimer Wyre Common Cleobury Mortimer 01299 271112	18 6450 27 holes Parkland	£17 Wd £20 We	Yes	Restaurant Bar Correct golfing dress
Hill Valley Golf & Country Club Terrick Rd Whitchurch 01948 663584	18 6050 Parkland		No	Catering Available
Meole Brace Meole Brace Shrewsbury 01743 364050	9 5830 Parkland		No	
Severn Meadows Highley Nr Bridgnorth 01746 862212	9 5258 Parkland		No	Catering Available Bar
The Shropshire Muxton Grange Muxton Telford 01952 677800	27 (3 x 9) Variable Terrain	£12 (18 holes) Wd £18 (18 holes) We	Yes	Full Catering Correct Dress

Name & Address	Holes/Yards Description	Green Fee	Driving Range	Facilities etc.
Cannington Cannington College Nr Bridgwater 01278 652394	9 2929 Parkland	£10 (18) Wd £12 (18) We	No	Restaurant Bar
Entry Hill Entry Hill Rd Bath 01225 834248	9 2103 Hilly Parkland	£4.50 Wd £5.40 We	No	
Frome Golf Centre Critchill Manor Frome 01373 453410	18/Par 69 5513 Parkland/ Meadowland	£10/£12 (18)Wd/We £7/£8 (9) Wd/We	Yes Floodlit Covered	Light Snacks Bar Soft Drinks
Halstock Common Lane Halstock, Nr Yeovil 01935 891689	18 4351 Parkland	£10 Wd £12 We	Yes	Light Snacks
Isle of Wedmore Lineage, Lascots Hill Wedmore 01934 712452	18 6000 Parkland	£18 Wd £22 We	No	Full Restaurant Bar Function Suite
Long Sutton Long Load Nr. Langport 01458 241017	18 6368 Parkland	£14 Wd £17 We	Yes	Restaurant Bar
Mangotsfield Carson's Rd Mangotsfield Bristol 0117 9565501	18 5300 Meadowland	£9 Wd £11 We	No	Catering Available
Mendip Spring Honeyhall Lane Congresbury Bristol 01934 853337	18 6328 Parkland	£17 Wd £19 We £6 (9)	Yes	Restaurant Bar
Oake Manor Oake Nr Taunton 01823 461993	18 6109 Parkland/ Lakes	£13.50 Wd £15 We	Yes	Restaurant Bar Bar Snacks
Puxton Park Woodspring Golf & Leisure Park Nr Weston-s-Mare 01934 876942	18 6559 Moorland	£8 Wd £10 We	No	Bar

Name & Address	Holes/Yards Description	Green Fee	Driving Range	Facilities etc.
Stockwood Vale Stockwood Lane Keynsham Bristol 0117 9866505	18 6031 Parkland	£12 Wd £14 We	Yes	Restaurant Bar Dress restrictions apply
Tall Pines Cooks Bridle Path Downside Nr Bristol 01275 472076	18 5857 Parkland	£12 Wd £14 We	No	Restaurant Bar
Tickenham Clevedon Rd Tickenham 01275 856626	9 4000 Parkland	£5 (9) Wd £7 (9) We £9/£10/ (18)	Yes Floodlit to 8.30pm	Catering / Bar Golf Shop PGA Lessons School
Vivary In the centre of Taunton 01823 289274	18 4620 Parkland	£7.50	No	Restaurant Bar
Wheathill Wheathill Nr. Somerton 01963 240667	18 5362 Parkland	£10 Wd £15 We	No	Full Catering Bar
Wincanton The Racecourse Wincanton 01963 34606	9 6218 Centre of Racecourse	£6 Wd £10 We	No	
Woodlands Woodlands Lane Almondsbury Bristol 01454 619319	18 6068 Parkland	£12 Wd £15 We	No	Full Catering
Woodspring Yanley Lane Long Ashton Bristol	27/2942 /3320 /3340 Parkland	£25 Wd £28.50 We	Yes	Full Catering Handicap Certs at Weekend
Yeovil Newton Yeovil Golf Club Sherborne Rd Yeovil 01935 422965	9 4891 Parkland	£15 Wd £18 We	No	Full Catering

Name & Address	Holes/Yards Description	Green Fee	Driving Range	Facilities etc.
Cannock Park Stafford Rd Cannock 01543 578850	18 5048 Parkland	£6.50 Wd £7.50 We	No	Full Catering
Goldenhill Mobberley Rd Goldenhill Stoke-on-Trent 01782 784715	18 5957 Parkland/ Meadowland	£6 Wd £7 We	No	Restaurant Bar
Himley Hall Golf Centre, Log Cabin Himley Hall Park Dudley 01902 895207	9 6215 Parkland	£5.50 Wd & We	No	Cafe
Newcastle Newcastle Rd Keele 01782 627596	18 6256 Parkland		Yes	Bar Meals Bar
Parkhall Hulme Rd Weston Coyney Stoke-on-Trent 01782 599584	18 2335 Moorland		No	
Perton Park Wrottesley Park Rd Perton Wolverhampton 01902 380073	18 6620 Meadowland	£10 Wd £15 We	Yes	Full Catering
Seedy Mill Elm Hurst Lichfield 01543 417333	18/6247 9 Par 3 Parkland	£16 Wd £22 We	No	Full Catering
Tamworth Eagle Drive Amington Tamworth 01827 53850	18 6605 Parkland	£8.50	No	Catering Available Bar
Three Hammers Golf Complex Old Stafford Rd Coven 01902 790428	18 Par 3		Yes	Restaurant Bar

Name & Address	Holes/Yards Description	Green Fee	Driving Range	Facilities etc.
Cretingham Cretingham Woodbridge 01728 685275	9 4552 Parkland	£9 per Wd (18) £11 We (18)	Yes	Full Catering Bar Swimming Pool Tennis/Snooker
Hintlesham Hall Hintlesham Ipswich 01473 652761	18 6638 Parkland	£27 Wd £27 We	Yes	Full Catering Golf: Book Ahead
St Helena Bramfield Rd Halesworth 01966 875567	18 6580 Parkland	£15 Wd £18 We	Yes	Full Catering
Seckford Seckford Hall Rd Great Bealings Woodbridge 01394 388000	18 Parkland	£13 Wd £15 Sun	Yes	Full Catering Golf : Book Ahead
Stonham Barns Golf Centre Stonham Barns Pettaugh Rd Stonham Aspel 01449 711545	9 2718 Parkland	£3.50/ Round £5/ Day Wd & We	Yes	Catering Available on Site
The Suffolk G & CC St John's Hill Plantn. The Street Fornham All Saints Bury St Edmunds 01284 706777	18 6209 Parkland	£10 Wd £15 We	No	Full Catering
Ufford Park Hotel Yarmouth Rd Ufford Woodbridge 01394 382836	18 6325 Parkland	£16 Wd £20 We	No	Full Catering Golf: Book Ahead

Name & Address	Holes/Yards Description	Green Fee	Driving Range	Facilities etc.
Abbey Moor Green Lane Addlestone Surrey 01932 570741	9 5164 Parkland	£7 Wd £8 We	No	Restaurant Bar
Addington Court Featherbed Lane Croydon 0181 6570281	18/5577 18/5513 9/1733 Heathland	£11.50/Wd £9.99/Wd £6.95/Wd	No	Full Catering
Bowenhurst Mill Lane Crondall Nr Farnham 01252 851695	9 2100 Parkland	£5 Wd £6.50 We	Yes	Snacks
Broadwater Park Guildford Rd Farncombe Nr Godalming 01483 429955	9 1287/Par 3 Parkland	£3.75 Wd £4.25 We	Yes	Snacks Bar
Chessington Garrison Lane Chessington 0181 9741705	9 1353 (Par 3) Parkland	£4 Wd £4.90 We	Yes	Full Catering
Chiddingfold Petworth Rd Chiddingfold 01428 685888	18 5482 Downland	£14 Wd £18 We	No	Full Catering
Hoebridge Golf Centre Old Woking Rd Old Woking 01483 722611	18/6536 9/2294 18/2230 Parkland	£16 £8 £7 Wd & We	Yes	Restaurant Snacks
Horton Park Country Club Hook Rd Epsom 1081 3938400	18 5100 Parkland		No	Restaurant Bars Golf Shoes No Jeans
Hurtmore Hurtmore Rd Hurtmore, Godalming 01483 426492	18 5514 Parkland	£10 Wd £15 We	No	Restaurant Bar Golf Shoes No Jeans
Moore Place Portsmouth Rd Esher 01372 463533	9 4186 Parkland	£5.50 Wd £7.40 We	No	Full Catering
Oak Park(Crondall) Heath Lane Crondall Nr Farnham 01252 850880	18 6318 Woodland 9/3279 Parkland	£18 Wd £25 We £8/£10 Wd/We/ (9)	Yes	Restaurant Bar

Name & Address	Holes/Yards Description	Green Fee	Driving Range	Facilities etc.
Oaks Sports Centre Woodmansterne Rd Carshalton 0181 6438363	18/6033 9/1590 Meadowland	£11 Wd £13 We/18 £4.50 Wd £5.50 We/9	Yes	Full Catering Bar
Pachesham Golf Centre Oaklawn Rd Leatherhead 01372 843453	9 5608 Parkland	£7.50 Wd £9 We	Yes	Restaurant Bar
Pine Ridge Golf Centre Old Bisley Rd Frimley Camberley 01276 20770	18 6458 Forested Course	£16 Wd £20 We	Yes	Restaurant Bar
Pyrford Warren Lane Pyrford, Woking 01483 723555	18 6230 Meadowland	£35 Wd £50 We	No	Full Catering
Roker Park Holly Lane Aldershot Rd Guildford 01483 236677	9 6074 Parkland	£6.50 Wd £8 We	Yes	Restaurant Bar
Rusper Rusper Road Newdigate 01293 871871	9 6218 Parkland	£11.50 (18) Wd £15.50 (18) We	Yes	Snacks Bar No jeans
Sandown Golf Centre More Lane Esher 01372 461234	9/5656 9/Par 3 Parkland	£5.50 Wd £7.25 We £3.40 Wd £4.25 We	Yes	Catering Available
Selsdon Park Hotel & Golf Club Sanderstead S. Croydon 0181 6578811	18 6429 Parkland	£15 Wd £25/day We	Yes	Full Catering
Shillinglee Park Chiddingfold Godalming 01428 663237	9 5032 Parkland	£11 Wd £13 We	No	Restaurant Bar
Windlemere Windlesham Rd West End Woking 01276 858727	9 2673 Parkland	£8 Wd £9.50 We	Yes	Snacks Bar

Name & Address	Holes/Yards Description	Green Fee	Driving Range	Facilities etc.
Avisford Park Yapton Lane Walberton Arundel, WS 01243 554611	9 5703 Parkland	£14 Wd £18 We	No	Bar
Brookfield Winterpit Lane Plummer's Plain Horsham, WS 01403 891568	9 4000 Parkland	£10	Yes	Restaurants Bars
Dewlands Manor Cottage Hill Rotherfield, ES 01892 852266	9 6372 (18 tees) Parkland/ Woodland	£13.00 (9) Wd £15.00 (9) We	No	Snacks Bar No jeans or trainers
Eastbourne Golfing Park Lottbridge Drove Eastbourne, ES 01323 520400	9 Lakeland	£8	Yes All - Weather Floodlit	Full Catering
Hassocks London Rd Hassocks, WS 01273 846630	18 5754 Parkland	£11.25 Wd £14.75 We	No	Full Catering
Hastings Battle Rd St Leonards-on-Sea, ES 01424 852981	18 6248 Parkland	£10.30 Wd £13 We	Yes	Full Catering
Hill Barn Hill Barn Lane Worthing, WS 01903 237301	18 5809 Downland	£11.50 Wd £13.50 We	No	Snacks, Hot Meals
Hollingbury Park Ditchling Rd Brighton, ES 01273 552010	18 6472 Downland	£11 Wd £15 We	No	Full Catering
Horam Park Chiddingly Rd Horam, ES 01435 813477	9 (18 tees) 5970 Parkland		Yes	Restaurant Bar
Horsham Golf Park Worthing Rd Horsham, WS 01403 271525	9 4122 Parkland	£6 (9) Wd £7 (9) We	Yes	Restaurant Bar
Osiers Farm Petworth, WS 01798 344097	9 5220 Farmland	£9	Yes	Light Refreshments

Name & Address	Holes/Yards Description	Green Fee	Driving Range	Facilities etc.
Pease Pottage GC Horsham Rd Pease Pottage Crawley, WS 01293 521706	9 3511 Parkland	£8.50 (18) Wd £11 (18) We	Yes	Restaurant Bar
Rustington Golf Centre Golfers Lane Rustington, WS 01903 850790	9 (18 tees) 5735 9 (Par 3) Parkland	£13.50 (18) Wd £15.50 (18) We	Yes	Coffee Shop Bar
Seaford Head Southdown Rd Seaford, ES 01323 894843	18 5848 Seaside	£11.50 Wd £14 We	No	Light Snacks
Sedlescombe (Aldershaw) Sedlescombe, ES 01424 870898	18 6500 Parkland	£12.50 Wd £14 We	Yes	Snacks Bar
Slinfold Park Golf & Country Club Stane St, Slinfold Horsham, WS 01403 791555	18/6418 9/1315 Parkland	£25 (18) £4 (9) Wd & We	Yes	Full Catering
Tilgate Forest Golf Centre Titmus Drive Tilgate, Crawley, WS 01293 530103	18/6359 9/1136 Parkland	£11.85 Wd £16.25 We	Yes	Restaurant Bar
Wellshurst Golf & Country Club North St Hellingly, ES 01435 813636	18 5771 Parkland	£14 Wd £17.50 We	Yes	Full Catering Bar
West Chiltington Broadford Bridge Rd West Chiltington, WS 01798 813574	18 5900 9 (par 3) Parkland	£13/£17.50 (18) £6.50/ £8.50 (9) Wd/We	Yes	Full Catering

Name & Address	Holes/Yards Description	Green Fee	Driving Range	Facilities etc.
Elemore Elemore Lane Hetton-le-Hole 0191 5269020	18 5947 Parkland	£6	No	Bar
Parklands High Gosforth Park Newcastle-upon-Tyne 0191 2364480	18 6664 Parkland	£17 Wd £25 We	Yes	Restaurant Bar

				WARWICKSHIRE
Name & Address	Holes/Yards Description	Green Fee	Driving Range	Facilities etc.
Ingon Manor Golf & Country Club Ingon Lane,Snitterfield Nr Stratford/Avon 01789 731857	18 6600 Parkland	£15 Wd £20 We	No	Full Catering
Lea Marston Hotel & Leisure Complex Haunch Lane Lea Marston 01675 470468	9 783 Par 3	£3 Wd £4.75 We	Yes	Restaurant Bars
Newbold Comyn Newbold Terrace East Leamington Spa 01926 421157	18 6315 Parkland	£8 Wd £10.50 We	No	Restaurant Bar
Warwick The Racecourse Warwick 01926 494316	9 2682 Meadowland	£4 Wd £5.50 We	Yes	Bar
Whitefields Coventry Rd Thurlaston Nr Rugby 01788 521800	18 6433 Parkland	£16 Wd £20 We	Yes	Restaurant Bars
Wishaw Bulls Lane Wishaw Sutton Coldfield 0121 3132110	18 5481 Parkland	£10 Wd £15 We	No	Full Catering

Name & Address	Holes/Yards Description	Green Fee	Driving Range	Facilities etc.
Ansty Golf Centre Brinklow Rd Ansty Coventry 01203 621341	18 5773 Parkland	£9 Wd £13 We	Yes	Full Catering Bar
Boldmere Monmouth Drive Sutton Coldfield 0121 3543379	18 4482 Parkland	£8 Wd £8.50 We	No	Catering Available
Brand Hall Heron Rd Oldbury, Warley 0121 5522195	18 5734 Parkland		No	Cafe Bar
Calderfields Golf Academy Aldridge Rd Walsall 01922 32243	18 6700 Parkland	£10 per round	Yes	Full Catering
City of Coventry (Brandon Wood) Brandon Lane Coventry 01203 543141	18 6610 Parkland	£9.15 Wd £12.20 We	Yes	Meals (Mar/Oct)
Cocks Moor Woods Alcester Rd South Kings Heath Birmingham 0121 4443584	18 5819 Parkland	£8 Wd £8.50 We	No	Catering Available
Corngreaves Corngreaves Rd Cradley Heath 01384 567880	9 Parkland		No	
Harbone Church Farm Vicarage Rd Harbone Birmingham 0121 4271204	9 4914 Parkland	£4.50 Wd £5 We	No	Snacks & Meals
Hatchford Brook Coventry Rd Sheldon Birmingham 0121 7439821	18 6202 Parkland	£8 Wd £8.50 We	No	Canteen
Hill Top Park Lane Handsworth Wood Birmingham 0121 5544463	18 6254 Parkland	£8 Wd £8.50 We	No	Catering Available

Name & Address	Holes/Yards Description	Green Fee	Driving Range	Facilities etc.
Lickey Hills (Rose Hill) Lickey Hills Rednal Birmingham 0121 4537600	18 6254 Parkland	£8.50	No	Snacks
Memorial Park Mem. Park Golf Office Leamington Rd Coventry 01203 675415	18 Par 3		No	Cafe in summer
Pype Hayes Eachelhurst Rd Walmley Sutton Coldfield 0121 3511014	18 5964 Parkland	£7.50 Wd £8.50 We	No	Cafeteria
Sedgley Golf Centre Sandyfields Rd Sedgley Dudley 01902 880503	9 3147	£5.50 Wd £6 We	Yes	Catering Available
Swindon Bridgnorth Rd Swindon, Dudley 01902 897031	18 6091 Wooded/ Parkland	£18 Wd £27 We	Yes	Restaurant Bar
Warley Lightwoods Hill Smethwick Warley 0121 4292440	9 2685 Parkland	£4.50 Wd £5.50 We	No	Catering Available
Wergs Keepers Lane Tettenhall Wolverhampton 01902 742225	18 6949 Parkland	£13.50 Wd £17 We	No	Restaurant Bar
Widney Manor Saintbury Drive Widney Manor Solihull 0121 7113646	18 5103 Parkland	£8 Wd £11.50 We	No	Full Catering
Windmill Village Hotel Birmingham Rd Allesley Coventry 01203 407241	18 5169 Flat/Hilly	£9.95 Wd £13.95 We	No	Catering Available

Name & Address	Holes/Yards Description	Green Fee	Driving Range	Facilities etc.
Brinkworth Longmans Farm Brinkworth Chippenham 01666 510277	18 5884 Meadowland	£6 Wd £8 We	No	Catering Available
Broome Manor Piper's Way Swindon 01793 532403	18 /6283 9/2690 Parkland	£10.50 (18) £6.50 (9)	Yes	Full Catering
Erlestoke Sands Erlestoke Devizes 01380 831069	18 6649 Parkland	£16 Wd £25 We	Yes	Full Catering
Highworth Golf Centre Swindon Rd Highworth 01793 766014	9 3120 Downland	£6.50	No	
Monkton Park Par 3 Monkton Park Chippenham 01249 653928	9 Par 3	9: £3/£3.20 18: £4.50/ £4.80 Wd/We	No	Refreshments Available
Oaksey Park Oaksey Nr. Malmesbury 01666 577996	9 2904 Parkland	£8 Wd £13 We	Yes	Full Catering
Shrivenham Park Pennyhooks Shrivenham Swindon 01793 783853	18 6100 Parkland	£10.50 Wd £12.50 We	No	Restaurant Bar
Thoulstone Park Chapmanslade Nr. Westbury 01373 832825	18 6312 Parkland	£18 Wd £24 We	Yes	Restaurant Bars

Name & Address	Holes/Yards Description	Green Fee	Driving Range	Facilities etc.
Abbey Park Golf & Country Club Dagnell End Rd Redditch 01527 63918	18 6411 Parkland	£10 Wd £12.50 We	Yes	Full Catering Bar
Bransford (Pine Lakes) Bank House Hotel Bransford Worcester 01886 833551	18 6101 Florida Style		Yes	Full Catering
Bromsgrove Golf Centre Stratford Rd Bromsgrove 01527 575886	9 5820 Meadowland	£6 Wd £7 We	No	Light Meals Bar
Ombersley Bishops Wood Rd Lineholt, Ombersley Droitwich 01905 620747	18 6139 Parkland	£10 Wd £13.30 We	Yes	Full Catering
Perdiswell Bilford Rd Worcester 01905 457189	9 2935 Meadowland	£4.30 Wd £5.70 We	No	Snacks Bar
Pitcheroak Plymouth Rd Redditch 01527 541054	9 4561 Parkland	£4.25 Wd £4.75 We	No	Restaurant Bar
Sapey Golf Upper Sapey Nr Worcester 01886 853288	18 5935 Parkland	£15 Wd £20 We	Yes	Snacks Mon & Tue Restaurant Wed-Sun
The Vale Golf & Country Club Hill Furze Rd Bishampton, Pershore 01386 462781	18/7114 9/2628 Parkland/ Downland	£18 £7.50	Yes	Full Catering
Wyre Forest Zortech Avenue Kidderminster 01299 822682	18 5790 Parkland	£9 Wd £12.50 We	Yes	Full Catering Bar

Name & Address	Holes/Yards Description	Green Fee	Driving Range	Facilities etc.
Boothferry Park Spaldington Lane Howden 01430 430364	18 6447 Meadowland	£9 Wd £14 We	No	Full Catering Bar
Bridlington Links Flamborough Rd Marton Bridlington 01262 401584	18/6719 9/1349 Clifftops Links	£10 Wd £12.50 We	Yes	Full Catering Bar
Cave Castle Hotel South Cave Brough 01430 421286	18 6409 Parkland	£12.50 Wd £18 We	No	Full Catering
Cherry Burton Leconfield Rd Cherry Burton Beverley 01964 550924	9 2278 Parkland	£5 Wd £6 We	No	Bar Snacks Bar
Cottingham Spring Park Farm Park Lane Cottingham 01482 842394	18 6230 Parkland	£12 Wd £18 We	Yes	Full Catering Bar
Spaldington Spaldington Lane Howden 01430 432484	9 1741 Parkland	£3.50	Yes	
Springhead Park Willerby Rd Hull 01482 656309	18 6402 Parkland	£7 Wd £8 We	No	Full Catering
Sutton Park Salthouse Rd Holderness Rd Hull 01482 374242	18 6251 Parkland	£6.50 Wd £8.50 We	No	Full Catering Bar

Name & Address	Holes/Yards Description	Green Fee	Driving Range	Facilities etc.
Forest of Galtres Moorlands Rd Skelton, York 01904 766198	18 6312 Parkland	£16 Wd £21 We	No	Full Catering Bar & Lounge
Forest Park Stockton on Forest York 01904 400425	27 holes 18/6660 9x2/6372 Parkland	£16/£21 (18) £8/£10 (9) Wd/We	Yes	Full Catering Bar
Hunley Hall Brotton Saltburn-by-the-Sea 01287 676216	18 6510 Coastal	£18 Wd £25 We	Yes	Full Catering Bars Accommodation
Middlesborough Municipal Ladgate Lane Middlesborough 01642 315533	18 6333 Parkland	£7.75 Wd £9.75 We	Yes	Catering Available Golf: Ring for tee times
Romanby Yafforth Rd Northallerton 01609 777824	18 6657 Parkland	£14 Wd £18 We	Yes	Full Catering
Rudding Park Follifoot Harrogate	18 6871 Parkland	£16 Wd £19 We	Yes	Full Catering
Swallow Hall Swallow Hall Crockey Hill York 01904 448889	18 3092/ Par3	£7 Wd £8 We	Yes	Coffee Machine Cold Drinks

Name & Address	Holes/Yards Description	Green Fee	Driving Range	Facilities etc.
Austerfield Park Cross Lane Austerfield Doncaster 01302 710841	18 6859 9/Par 3 Parkland	£17 Wd £21 We 9/£2	Yes	Restaurant Bar Bar Snacks Par 3
Barnsley Wakefield Rd Staincross Nr Barnsley 01226 382856	18 6042 Parkland	£7.50 Wd £8.50 We	No	Bar Meals
Beauchief Abbey Lane Sheffield 0114 2620040	18 5452 Meadowland	£8 Wd £8.70 We	No	Catering Available
Birley Wood Birley Lane Sheffield 0114 2647262	18 5088	£7.75 Wd £8.10 We	No	
Crookhill Park Conisbrough Nr Doncaster 01709 862979	18 5839 Parkland	£8.25 Wd £9.50 We	No	Bar Snacks Bar
Grange Park Upper Wortley Rd Rotherham 01709 559497	18 6421 Parkland	£8 Wd £9.50 We	No	Catering Available
Lakeside Rother Valley Mansfield Rd Wales Bar, Sheffield 0114 2473000	18/6602 9 / Par 3 Parkland	£8 Wd £14 We	Yes	Restaurant Bar
Robin Hood Owston Hall Owston Doncaster 01302 722800	18 6937 Parkland	£10 Wd £14 We	No	Catering Bar Dress Restrictions
Sandhill c/o Colliery Farm Little Houghton Barnsley 01226 753444	18 6214 Meadowland	£8 Wd £10 We	Yes	Full Catering
Thorne Kirton Lane Thorne Doncaster 01405 812084	18 5366 Parkland	£8.75 Wd £9.75 We	No	Full Catering

Name & Address	Holes/Yards Description	Green Fee	Driving Range	Facilities etc.
Tinsley Park High Hazel Park Darnall Sheffield 0114 2560237	18 6103 Parkland	£7.75 Wd £8.10 We	No	Full Catering
Wombwell (Hillies) Wentworth View Wombwell Barnsley 01226 754433	9 4190 Meadowland	£3 Wd £3.70 We	No	Bar (Evenings & Weekends)

Name & Address	Holes/Yards Description	Green Fee	Driving Range	Facilities etc.
Bradley Park Bradley Rd Huddersfield 01484 223772	18/6220 9/ Par 3 Parkland	£11 Wd £13 We	Yes	Full Catering
Brandon Holywell Lane Shadwell Leeds 0113 2737471	18 3601 Parkland	£5 Wd £6 We	No	Catering Available Golf: Correct Footwear. Set of clubs each
City of Wakefield Lupset Park Horbury Rd Wakefield 01924 360282	18 6419 Parkland	£8 Wd £10 We	No	Catering for Groups by Arrangement
Crow Nest Park Coach Rd Brighouse 01422 201216	9 6020 Parkland	£8/£9 Wd/We (9) £13/£16 Wd/We(18)	Yes	Full Catering Dress Code No jeans Own clubs
Fardew Nursery Farm Carr Lane E. Morton, Keighley 01274 561229	9 6208 Parkland	£6 Wd £7 We/9 £10 Wd £12 We/18	No	
Leeds Golf Centre Wike Ridge Lane Shadwell, Leeds 0113 2886186	18/6620 12/1350 Par 3 Heathland	£10 Wd £12.50 We £5/12 All Days	Yes	Full Catering
Lofthouse Hill Leeds Rd Lofthouse, Wakefield 01924 823703	18 Links Style	£10 Wd £15 We	Yes	Restaurant Bars
Middleton Park Ring Rd Beeston, Leeds 0113 2700449	18 5263 Parkland	£7.50	No	
Oulton Park Rothwell Leeds 0113 2823152	18/6479 9/3287 Parkland	£10 (18 holes) £5 (9 holes)	Yes	Catering Available Bar
Pontefract Park Park Rd, Pontefract 01977 702799	9 2034 Parkland	£2.50	No	
Roundhay Park Lane Leeds 0113 2661686	9 5322 Parkland	£7.50 Wd £8.50 We	No	Catering Available Evenings Tues/Sat

Name & Address	Holes/Yards Description	Green Fee	Driving Range	Facilities etc.
Scathingwell Scathingwell Centre Scathingwell Tadcaster 01937 557878	18 6700 Parkland	£15 Wd £17 We	No	Catering Available Bar
The Shay Grange Golf Centre, Long Lane Off Bingley Rd Bradford 01274 491945	9 1650 Parkland	£6 (9) £10 (18)	Yes	Catering Bar Available
Springmill Queens Drive Osset 01924 272515	9 1165/ Par 3 Parkland		No	
Swingtime (Leeds) Redcote Lane Leeds 0113 2633030	9 2734 Parkland		Yes	Full Catering
Temple Newsam Temple Newsam Rd Leeds 0113 2645624	18/6153 18/6094 Parkland		No	Catering W/e Bar (7days)
Whitwood Altofts Lane Whitwood Castleford 01977 512835	9 6282 Parkland	£5.40 Wd £6.95 We	No	
Willow Valley Golf & Country Club Highmoor Lane Clifton, Brighouse 01274 878624	18/6988 9/2039 Parkland	£15 £9	Yes	Catering Available Bar
Woolley Park Woolley Wakefield 01226 390144	18 5900 Old Parkland	£10 Wd £15 We	No Practice Area	

Name & Address	Holes/Yards Description	Green Fee	Driving Range	Facilities etc.
Auchterderran Woodend Rd Cardenden 01592 721579	9 5250 Parkland	£9 Wd £12.50 We	No	Snacks Meals to order Bar
Ballingry Lochore Meadows Country Park Crosshill, Ballingry 01592 860086	9 6484 Parkland	£5.80 Wd £8.40 We	No	Catering Available in Centre
Braid Hills Braid Hills Approach Road Edinburgh 0131 4529408	18/5731 18/4832 Hillside	£7.40	No	Catering by Arrangement
Caird Park Mains Loan Dundee 01382 453606	18 6303 Parkland	£12.40 Wd £20.60 We	No	Catering by Arrangement Bar
Carrickknowe Glendevon Park Edinburgh 0131 3371096	18 6299 Meadowland	£7.40	No	Catering by Arrangement
Colonsay Isle of Colonsay 01951 200316	18 4775 Machair	£5 per annum No green fees	No	
Cowdenbeath Seco Place Cowdenbeath Nr Dunfermline 01383 511918	9 6552 Parkland	£6.50 Wd £9.25 We	No	Snacks Bar
Craigentinny 143 Craigentinny Ave Edinburgh 0131 5547501	18 5413 Links	£7.40	No	Catering by Arrangement
Craignure Scallastle Isle of Mull 01680 812487	9 5072 Links	£11 per day	No	
Dalmally Old Saw Mill Dalmally 01838 200370	9 2277 Parkland	£8 per day	No	Catering by Arrangement
Glenrothes Golf Course Rd Glenrothes 01592 754561	18 6444 Parkland	£12	No	Full Catering

Name & Address	Holes/Yards Description	Green Fee	Driving Range	Facilities etc.
Grangemouth Polmonthill Polmont 01324 711500	18 6314 Parkland	£6 Wd £7.60 We	No	Catering by Arrangement
Green Hotel Beaches Park Kinross 01577 863467	18/6257 18/6456 Parkland	£15 Wd £25 We	No	Catering Available
Inverary Inverary 01499 302508	9 5700 Parkland	£10 per day	No	
Kinghorn Macduff Crescent Kinghorn 01592 890978	18 5269 Links	£9 Wd £12 We	No	Catering by Arrangement
North Inch adj. Gannochy Trust Sports Complex (North of Perth) 01738 636481	9 5178 Parkland	£5.25 Wd £7.50 We	No	Catering in Sports Complex Flood Defence Work 1999/2000
Polkemmet Country Park, Park Centre Whitburn Bathgate 01501 743905	9 2969 Parkland	£3.40 Wd £4.20 We	Yes	Full Catering Bar
Portobello Stanley St Portobello Edinburgh 0130 6694361	9 4810 Parkland	£3.70	No	
St Andrews Links Management Committee Pilmour Cottage St Andrews 01334 475757	New Course 18/6604 Jubilee 18/6223 Eden 18/5588 Balgove 9/1399 Strathtyrum 18/5094 Duke's 18/6039	Apply for Details	No	Many Local Hotels
Vogrie Vogrie Estate Country Park Gorebridge 01875 821716	9 2530 Parkland	£5.40	No	Tearoom

Name & Address	Holes/Yards Description	Green Fee	Driving Range	Facilities etc.
Alford Montgarrie Rd Alford 019755 62178	18 5483 Parkland	£12 Wd £19 We	No	Catering Available Bar
Auchmill Bonny View Auchmill, Aberdeen 01224 714577	18 5560	£4.45	No	
Balnagask St Fitticks Rd Balnagask, Aberdeen 01224 876407	18 5986 Seaside	£4.45 Winter £6.30 Summer	No	Catering by Arrangement with Council
Banchory Kinneskie Rd Banchory 01330 822365	18 5481 Parkland	£18 Wd £21 We	No	Full Catering
Durness Balnakeil Durness 01971 511364	9 (18 tees) 5555 Seaside	£12 per day	No	Snacks (May - Sept)
Hazlehead Hazlehead Park Aberdeen 01224 317336	18/6045 18/6304 9/2770 Moorland	£6.85 (18 holes)	No	
King's Links Aberdeen 01224 632269	18 6384 Seaside		No	
Lybster Main Street Lybster	9 1898 Moorland		No	
Newtonmore Golf Course Rd Newtonmore 01540 673328	18 6029 Moorland/ Parkland	£10 Wd £14 We	No	Catering Available (not Tues)
Northern Golf Rd Kings Links Aberdeen 01224 636440	18 6270 Seaside	£7.20	No	Catering By Arrangement
Stromness Ness Stromness Orkney 01856 850772	18 4762 Parkland	£12 per day	No	Bar

Name & Address	Holes/Yards Description	Green Fee	Driving Range	Facilities etc.
Torvean Glenurquhart Rd Inverness 01463 711434 (Starter)	18 5784 Parkland	£9 Wd £11 We	No	Catering by Arrangement Golf: Booking Advisable
Traigh Traigh Farm Arisaig 01687 450645	9 2405 Links	£6 per day	No	Snacks
Whalsay Skaw Taing Island of Whalsay, Shetland 01806 566481	18 6009 Moorland/ Parkland	£5	No	Snacks Bar

Name & Address	Holes/Yards Description	Green Fee	Driving Range	Facilities etc.
Alexandra Park Golf Alexandra Park Sannox Gardens Glasgow 0141 5561294	9 2800 Hilly Parkland		No	
Auchenharvie Golf Complex Moor Park Rd West Brewery Pk,Stevenston 01294 603103	9 (18 tees) 2565 Links/ Parkland	£3.30 Wd £5.50 We	Yes	Bar
Barshaw Barshaw Park Glasgow Rd Paisley 0141 8892908	18 5703 Meadowland	£6	No	
Biggar The Park Broughton Rd Biggar 01899 220319	18 5537 Parkland	£8 per round/ Wd £10 per round /We	No	Full Catering Golf: Smart casual dress, no jeans
Caprington Ayr Rd Kilmarnock 01563 523702	18 5718 Parkland		No	By Arrangement
Castle Douglas Abercromby Rd Castle Douglas 01556 502801	9 5408 Parkland	£12	No	Bar in summer
Clydebank Overtoun Overtoun Rd Clydebank 0141 9526372	18 5643 Parkland	£4.40 Wd £4.80 Sun	No	Cafe
Coatbridge Townhead Rd Coatbridge 01236 428975	18 6026 Parkland		Yes	Full Catering
Dalmilling Westwood Ave Ayr 01292 263893	18 5752 Meadowland	£10	No	Light Meals Bar
Dalmuir Municipal Overtoun Rd Dalmuir Clydebank 0141 9528698	18 5349 Parkland		No	Cafe

Name & Address	Holes/Yards Description	Green Fee	Driving Range	Facilities etc.
Deaconsbank Stewarton Rd Thornliebank Glasgow 0141 6387044	18 4800 Parkland		Yes	Full Catering
Doon Valley Hillside Park Patna 01292 531607	9 5700 Meadowland	£5.35	No	Catering by Arrangement Bar
Gatehouse Laurieston Rd Gatehouse-of-Fleet 01644 450260	9 5042 Undulating	£10 Wd & We	No	
Gretna Kirtle View Gretna 01461 338464	9 3214 Parkland	£8 Wd £10 We/18 £5/9 holes	Yes	Meals Bar
Irvine Ravenspark 13 Kidsneuk Lane Irvine 01294 271293	18 6429 Parkland	£6.60 Wd £11 We £11/£16.50 /day	No	Lunches High Teas Bar
Larkhall Burnhead Rd Larkhall 01698 881113	9 6423	£3.75	No	Bar
Lethamhill Cumbernauld Rd Glasgow 0141 7706220	18 5836	£6.20 Summer £5.50 Winter	No	
Linn Park Simshill Rd Glasgow 0141 6375871	18 4952 Parkland	£6.20 Summer £5.50 Winter	No	
Littlehill Auchinaim Rd Bishopbriggs Glasgow 0141 7721916	18 6228 Parkland	£6.20 Summer £5.50 Winter	No	Lunches/not Mon
Maybole Memorial Park Maybole	9 2652 Hillside	£7 £11/day	No	

Name & Address	Holes/Yards Description	Green Fee	Driving Range	Facilities etc.
Ruchill Brassey St Maryhill Glasgow 0141 7700519	9 2240 Parkland		No	
Strathclyde Park Mote Hill Hamilton 01698 266155	9 3175 Parkland	£2.50	Yes	
Torrance House Strathaven Rd East Kilbride Glasgow 01355 248638	18 6640 Parkland	£16	No	Catering Available
Troon Municipal Harling Drive Troon 01292 312464	18/6687 18/6327 18/4784 Links		No	Full Catering
Vaul Scannish Isle of Tiree 01879 220562	9 6300 Seaside		No	
Westerwood Hotel, Golf & Country Club St Andrews Drive Cumbernauld 01236 452772	18 6721 Parkland	£22.50 Wd £27.50 We	Yes	Full Catering
Whinhill Beith Rd Greenock 01475 721064	18 5434 Parkland		No	

Name & Address	Holes/Yards Description	Green Fee	Driving Range	Facilities etc.
Mid Wales Golf Centre Maesmawr Caersws Nr Newtown 01686 688303	9 Par 3 1277 Meadowland	£6 Wd £8 We	Yes	Light Refreshments Bar
Old Rectory Hotel Llangattock Crickhowell 01873 810373	9 2360 Parkland	£5 Wd £5 We	No	Restaurant Bar Pool
Rhosgoch Rhosgoch Builth Wells 01497 851251	9 4842 Parkland	£7 Wd £10 We	No	Snacks Dinner by arrangement Bar
Summerhill Hereford Rd Clifford Hay-on-Wye 01497 820451	9 5825 Parkland	£8 Wd £10 We	No	Full Catering
Welsh Border Golf Complex Bulthy Farm, Bulthy Middletown Nr Welshpool 01743 884247	9/3006 9/1614 Par 3 Parkland	£7 £4	Yes	Restaurant Bar

Name & Address	Holes/Yards Description	Green Fee	Driving Range	Facilities etc.
Bala Lake Hotel Bala 01678 520344	9 4281 Parkland		No	Full Catering
Bryn Morfydd Hotel Llanrhaeadr Nr Denbigh 01745 890280	18/5850 9/1200 Parkland	£12 Wd £16 We	No	Full Catering
Caerwys Nine of Clubs Caerwys Mold 01352 720692	9 3088 Parkland	£4.50 Wd (18 holes) £5.50 We (18 holes)	No	Light Refreshments
Chirk Chirk Nr Wrexham 01691 774407	18 7045 Parkland	£15 Wd £22 We	Yes	Full Catering
Clay's Farm Golf Centre Bryn Estyn Rd Wrexham 01978 661406	18 5624 Parkland	£11 Wd £14 We	No	Full Catering
Kimnel Park Golf Complex Bodelwyddan 01745 833548	9 Par 3	from £3/round	Yes	Restaurant Bar Night-time golf
Llangefni Anglesey 01248 722193	9 1467 Parkland	£2.20	No	
Llanerch Park N. Wales Golf Range & Course Llanerch Pk, St Asaph 01745 730805	9 1587 Parkland	£2	Yes	Light Refreshments
Northop Country Park Northop Nr Chester 01352 840440	18 6735 Parkland	£25 Wd £35 We	No	Restaurant Bar
Penrhos Golf & CC Llanrhystud Nr Aberystwyth 01974 202999	18/6641 9/1827 Parkland	£15 Wd £18 We	Yes	Full Catering
Plassey Eyton Wrexham 01978 780020	9 2300 Parkland	£4 Wd £5 We	No	Full Catering

Name & Address	Holes/Yards Description	Green Fee	Driving Range	Facilities etc.
Alice Springs Bettws Newydd Usk 01873 880772	18/6041 18/6868 Parkland	£12.50 Wd £15 We	No	Full Catering Bar Golf: Phone Weekends
Allt-y-Graban Allt-y-Graban Rd Pontlliw Swansea 01792 885757	9 Parkland	£7 Wd £8 We (18 holes)	No	Catering Available
Caerleon Broadway Caerleon Newport 01633 420342	9 3092 Parkland	£3.90 Wd £4.10 We	Yes	Snacks
Castell Heights Blaengwynlais Caerphilly 01222 886666	9 2688 Mountainside		Yes	Snacks Bar
Celtic Manor Catsash Rd Coldra Woods Newport 01633 413000	18/7001 18/4094 Parkland		No	Full Catering Golf Academy
Coed-y-Mwster The Club House Coychurch Nr Bridgend 01656 862121	9 (12 tees) 5758 Parkland	£15 (18 holes)	No	Bar Meals all day Bar
Dewstow Caerwent Monmouthshire 01291 430444	18/6176 18/6123 Parkland	£13 Wd £16 We £20/day Mon/Fri	Yes	Full Catering Bars Corporate Societies
Earlswood Jersey Marine Neath 01792 321578	18 Parkland	£8	No	
Gower Cefn Goleu Three Crosses Gowerton, Swansea 01792 872480	18 6441 Parkland	£14 Wd £16 We	No	Full Catering
Greenmeadow Treherbert Rd Croesyceiliog Cwmbran 01633 869321	18 6300 Parkland		No	Full Catering

Name & Address	Holes/Yards Description	Green Fee	Driving Range	Facilities etc.
Inco Clydach Swansea 01792 844216	18 Parkland		No	Snacks Bar (Evenings)
Lakeside Water St Margam, Port Talbot 01639 899959	18 4400 Parkland	£10 Wd & We	Yes	Full Catering
Llanyrafon Llanfrechfa Way Cwmbran 01633 874636	9 Par 3	£2.30 Wd £3.15 We	No	
Oakdale Llwynon Lane Oakdale 01495 220044	9 1344 Parkland	£3.75 Wd & We	Yes	Snacks
Peterstone Golf & Country Club Peterstone Wentlooge Cardiff 01633 680009	18 6555 Seaside Parkland	£16.50 Wd £22.50 We	No	Restaurant Bar
Priskilly Forest Castle Morris Haverfordwest 01348 840276	9 5712 Parkland	£7 (9 holes) £10 (18 holes)	No	Catering on request Bar Snacks Accommodation
Raglan Parc Parc Lodge Raglan 01291 690077	18 6604 Parkland	£15/day Wd £20/day We	No	Light Meals Snacks Bar
The Rolls of Monmouth The Hendre Monmouth 01600 715353	18 6733 Parkland	£30 Wd £35 We £25 Mon (inc coffee & lunch)	No	Full Catering
St Andrews Major Coldbrook Rd East Nr Cadoxton Barry 01446 722227	9 5862 Parkland	£8 (9 holes) £13 (18 holes)	No	Restaurant Bar
South Pembrokeshire Military Rd Pennar Pembroke Dock 01646 621453	18 5804 Seaside Parkland	min £16	Yes	Meals - Restaurant (not Mondays)
Wernddu Golf Centre Abergavenny 01873 856223	9/ Par 31 9/ Par 36 Parkland	£6 (9 holes) £10 (18 holes)	Yes	Snacks Bar

INDEX

If you have any recommendations for Courses which might be included in the next edition of *"Easy Access* Golf Courses", or know of changes which should be made to any current entry, the publishers would be grateful if you would note the details in a photocopy of the boxes below and send to:

The Forge Press,
The Old Forge, Holton,
Wincanton, Somerset, UK, BA9 8AX

Name & Address	Holes/Yards Description	Green Fee	Driving Range	Facilities etc.